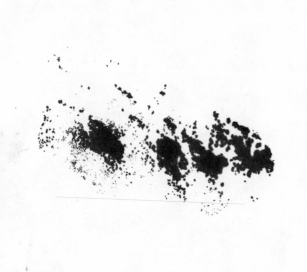

Take a trip to
SCOTLAND

Keith Lye
General Editor
Henry Pluckrose

Franklin Watts

London   New York   Sydney   Toronto

Facts about Scotland

Area:
78,772 sq. km.
(30,416 sq. miles)

Population:
5,116,000 (1981 census)

Capital:
Edinburgh

Largest cities:
Glasgow (762,000);
Edinburgh (419,000);
Aberdeen (190,000);
Dundee (174,000)

Official language:
English

Religion:
Christianity

Main products:
Oil, natural gas, coal,
engineering goods, ships,
electronic equipment,
textiles, whisky, fish,
cereals, timber

Currency:
Pound

Franklin Watts Limited
12a Golden Square
London W1

ISBN: UK Edition 0 86313 161 1
ISBN: US Edition 0-531-04873-X
Library of Congress Catalog
Card No: 84-50612

© Franklin Watts Limited 1984

Typeset by Ace Filmsetting Ltd,
Frome, Somerset
Printed in Hong Kong

Text Editor: Brenda Williams

Maps: Tony Payne

Design: Peter Benoist

Stamps: Stanley Gibbons Limited

Photographs: Scottish Tourist Board;
Zefa, 6, 7, 13, 14, 16, 23, 26; Chris
Fairclough, 18, 20, 21; Topham
Picture Library, 5, 7
Front cover: Topham Picture Library
Back cover: Chris Fairclough

Scotland is the most northerly part of
the United Kingdom of Great
Britain and Northern Ireland. It
joined England and Wales to form
Great Britain in 1707. Parts of
Scotland are wild and mountainous.
Ben Nevis is Britain's highest
mountain at 1,343 m (4,406 ft).

Scotland has many lochs, but some of these lakes are really deep inlets of the sea. Beautiful Loch Lomond, near Glasgow, is the largest lake in Great Britain.

Does "Nessie," a huge monster, live in Loch Ness in northern Scotland? Pictures like this may make us think that it does. But scientists do not agree about Nessie. Nobody has yet proved that the Loch Ness Monster exists.

Glasgow is Scotland's largest city.
It stands on the River Clyde, at the
heart of the west Central Lowlands.
The city has many industries and is
also important for business and the
arts.

Edinburgh is Scotland's capital city. Its most famous building is the castle. Scotland has many laws of its own, but no separate parliament. Its 72 Members of Parliament belong to the House of Commons in London. Scotland is divided into nine Regions and three Island Areas.

The picture shows some stamps and money used in Scotland. The main unit of currency is the pound. The coins are the same as those used in the rest of the United Kingdom.

Scotland

Orkney
Islands
•Kirkwall

NORTH
SEA

Shetland
Islands
•Lerwick

LEWIS
•Stornaway

Outer Hebrides

HARRIS

North West   *Highlands*

SCOTLAND

Inner Hebrides

SKYE

•Inverness

Loch Ness

Spey

Aviemore•

•Aberdeen

Glen More   *Cairngorm Mts*   *Dee*

•Balmoral

Ben
Nevis▲
1,343

Grampian Mountains

•Dundee

•Perth   •St Andrews

*Loch
Lomond*

Firth of Forth

•Glasgow   Edinburgh•

Clyde

ATLANTIC
OCEAN

•Ayr

Southern Uplands

North Channel

Dumfries•

IRELAND

ENGLAND

9

The Orkney Islands of northern
Scotland are one of the three Island
Areas. Here, fishing and farming are
important. North of the Orkneys are
the Shetland Islands. These have
become important in recent years as
a result of the North Sea oil industry.

The Western Isles form another Island Area. The Outer Hebrides are part of this group. They include Harris, the island where the famous Harris tweed is woven. Few people live in the islands and Highlands of Scotland.

The Inner Hebrides include Skye.
Ferry services from such places as
Kyleakin link Skye to the mainland.
Farming and fishing are now less
important on Skye. But tourism is
becoming a leading industry.

The Southern Uplands of Scotland are known for their sheep. Some crops are also grown there. But the chief farming region is the fertile Central Lowlands, which separate the Southern Uplands from the Highlands.

Loch Tay lies at the foot of Ben Lawers in Tayside Region. There are farms in the sheltered Highland valleys, or glens. Scotland produces barley, hay, potatoes, sugar-beet and wheat. It is also famous for its cattle.

Aberdeen is in northern Scotland and is the country's main fishing port. So many houses are built of granite that it is called the "Granite City." Here, a fisherman shows off a huge catch.

Glasgow is one of Europe's greatest industrial cities. There are coal mines nearby, and steel plants like this one are important. Metal goods, machinery and cloth are made here.

The River Clyde rises in the Southern Uplands and flows 170 km (106 miles) to the sea. Oceangoing ships sail up the Clyde to Glasgow's docks. Glasgow is a great port. Many ships were once made in Glasgow, but this industry is now less busy.

Scottish whisky is world famous. Much of it is made in Glasgow distilleries. Its special taste comes from two ingredients – the local water and malt, which has been cured over peat fires.

The Forth Road Bridge crosses the
Firth of Forth. It was opened in 1964
and links two parts of the Central
Lowlands where many people live. At
2.5 km (1.55 miles) long, it is one of
the world's longest suspension
bridges.

Travel is difficult in the wild Highlands of Scotland. The Caledonian Canal provides a short route between the east and west coast. It runs along the valley of Glen More linking canals and lakes, including Loch Ness.

Holyroodhouse is a royal palace in Edinburgh. It was the home of Mary, Queen of Scots, from 1561 to 1567. Bonnie Prince Charlie also stayed here. In 1745 he led a revolt of Highlanders who wanted him as king. The revolt ended in defeat in 1746.

Edinburgh holds a festival of music and drama every year. One event is the floodlit Edinburgh Tattoo, held in the Castle. Many Scottish soldiers take part, often wearing kilts. They march to the music of bagpipes.

Balmoral Castle is in northern Scotland, about 80 km (50 miles) west of Aberdeen. Queen Victoria and her husband Prince Albert bought the castle in 1853. It has been a home of the Royal Family ever since.

Famous Scottish writers include Sir Walter Scott, who lived at Abbotsford in the Southern Uplands. Other writers are R. L. Stevenson, whose *Treasure Island* is famous, and J. M. Barrie, who wrote *Peter Pan*.

Robert Burns (1759–1796) is Scotland's most famous poet and song-writer. Burns Night is held on January 25, his birthday. At this party, one man holds the musical instrument called a bagpipe. Another carries a haggis, a national dish.

Highland folk dancing takes place at Braemar near Balmoral. Dances include Scottish reels and the Highland fling. Highlanders keep many old customs. About 82,600 people still speak Gaelic, the ancient Scottish language. Most live in the Highlands and islands.

Aviemore lies in the valley of the River Spey, which cuts through the Highlands. In summer, people come for hammer-throwing and other sports. Traditional sports include tossing the caber – a thick wooden pole.

The Royal and Ancient Golf Club was founded at St. Andrews in 1754. Golf started in Scotland. The British Open Championship, the most important golf tournament in Britain, has been played at St. Andrews many times. St. Andrews also has Scotland's oldest University.

Soccer is a popular game in Scotland, especially in and around Glasgow. Glasgow has two important clubs, Celtic and Rangers. These clubs have always been keen rivals.

Southern and central Scotland
have a mild climate. The Highlands
are cold and snowy in winter.
Aviemore is the leading place for
winter sports in Britain. There are
ski schools for beginners.

Aberdeen is an ancient city. In recent years it has become important as western Europe's leading base for oil exploration. The North Sea oil industry has brought jobs to Scotland. Other new industries are also being developed, especially in the Central Lowlands.

Index